Contents

Cover photo: Crucifixion *by Albrecht Aldorfer (1480-1538) at Abbey of St. Fabian; photo credit by Eric Lessing/Art Resource, NY*

Introduction

If you were "bound for Golgotha," going on the journey that would take you to the place of Jesus' crucifixion, and beyond that, to his resurrection, what would you need to take along on the trip? I know the question is somewhat strange; but as you open this book and participate in this study, you are invited to take the journey with Jesus to Golgotha. Lent is more than the passing of 40 days plus seven Sundays. It is more than a movement from the middle of winter to the beginning of spring. Lent is a passage of spiritual time in which we engage our hearts and minds in a journey that can profoundly change us.

The journey to Golgotha will stretch us. It is a journey that will take us to a different place than where we normally live. On this journey, we will consider and talk about things in the midst of our everyday lives that are holy, powerful, and life-transforming. The jour ney invites us to look at the life of Jesus, at those who came before him, and at the thoughts and words of those who followed him. The journey will require that we take time to linger in the Scripture, to consider the questions and the answers that are offered, and to allow ourselves to be remade as the followers of Jesus Christ.

So the question remains: What would we need to take on this Lenten journey? Our discussion over these coming weeks provides some of the tools and experiences needed to move toward the Easter celebration. We will study words such as *promise, hope, new, transformation,* and *trust.* We will study prophecies of Isaiah and look at the covenant God made with Abraham and with the children of Israel. We will hear Paul's insights about Jesus Christ and about faith as found in Romans, Philippians, and Corinthians. We will move through the sweep of Jesus' life as found in Luke and arrive on Easter morning at the garden described in John's Gospel. My hope for you is that these sessions will be a guide to your growth in faith. Please be in prayer as you begin the journey!

All in This Together

Scriptures for Lent:
The First Sunday
Deuteronomy 26:1-11
Romans 10:8b-13
Luke 4:1-13

When our son Aaron was all of four years old, our family made the cross-country trip from North Dakota to Texas to visit my parents. Wise parents that we are, we found that the best traveling was to get up at a horribly early time, tuck the boys in their car seats, and drive until about two in the afternoon, when we would stop for the day at a hotel with a swimming pool. To get enough miles behind us, it sometimes meant getting into the car in the middle of the night and driving half the day before breakfast. Our second morning of driving had the adults awake at 2:30 A.M. and in the car at 2:45 A.M. to really get some miles in! As we placed the sleeping bundles of boys in their seats, Aaron woke up just long enough to raise his fist in the air and shout, "Fort Worth or Bust!" and then dropped back to sleep.

In a sense, that's our call for these holy and important weeks of 2007, "Easter or Bust!" as we take the Lenten road trip through the spiritual night, looking for Easter morning and the promise fulfilled. It is critical for us to realize, however, that as we make this trip, whether driving or riding sleepily in the back seat throughout the season, that we do so together. Lent is a trip for the community of faith. Many of our Scriptures for Lent, and especially the ones set apart for this week's study, speak to the communal efforts of growth, remembrance, and holy acts of worship.

REMEMBER WHO YOU ARE
DEUTERONOMY 26:1-11

I was leading a church camp with another pastor one summer. We needed to get a piece of equipment repaired and to purchase some supplies. We drove to the nearby town, and we found a repair shop. We explained the problem with the equipment, and the person in the repair shop said it could be fixed in a few hours. I was getting ready to give him the information about who we were and where we could be contacted when he said, "And this is Greg, and you must be Randy." Having never met the person before, I was amazed that he could correctly tell us our own names! I was amazed, that is, until I noticed him grinning. I looked down and realized that we were wearing our little wooden nametags from the church camp, hanging by laces around our necks. I am glad we had not gone to town to rob a bank!

I wish I could count the number of nametags I have been given, worn, lost, forgotten to take off, or saved in drawers throughout the years. Of course, the nametags are not for my benefit. They help those who need to know who I am. However, every time I get a nametag, I end up looking at it for a moment and thinking about that name that belongs to me, that identifies me, and that has made me part of who I am.

The ritual of the first fruits laid out in Deuteronomy 26 is a fascinating moment in the history of Israel. As the nation prepared to make its home in Canaan and to begin to enjoy the fruits of the land after so long wandering in the wilderness, Moses gave instructions. As they collected the first fruits of the harvest, they were to do so as a preparation for worship. They were instructed to take the harvest gleanings to the worship place, to set it before the priest who would set it before the altar, and then to make the affirmation of faith. It begins: "A wandering Aramean was my ancestor." They were to recount the history of the people in slavery in Egypt, freed by God's hand and mighty acts, and led through the wilderness to the land flowing with milk and honey.

The first fruit was an offering to God not only for what God had done but also for creating the people of Israel in this unique way. In essence, they were called to remember who they were. Imagine how powerful it would have been to hear the same words spoken thousands of times over as each person brought those first fruits: "A wandering Aramean was my ancestor." The Israelite people were wanderers until they found their home with God in the Promised Land. Even then, their wandering took them away from God's presence time and time again; and it was important for the worship to bring them back in touch with just exactly who they were and Whose they were. The first fruits were placed before the Lord God as an offering that helped the children of Israel to remember time and time again.

So worship reconnects us with the God who has never left us alone. In the ritual of the first fruits, Israel was reminded of their place and their relationship with God; and with that remembrance, they came to understand that all they were was a gift from God.

What a perfect way for us to begin our Lenten journey. The ritual of Ash Wednesday invites us to "remember that you are dust, and to dust you shall return." It also, however, reconnects us with God who created us out of the dust of the earth. It is as if, at the beginning of Lent, we are given new nametags to wear throughout the journey of this season.

Perhaps you can recount your own call to faith or those different experiences in which you can remember that God carried you. Perhaps if you wrote your faith history, you would include the stories told you by your parents or grandparents about the meaning of their faith. On the other hand, if you have children, do they know your faith story? Could they tell others about how God saw you through your own life? I recall that I met my wife, Cheri, the first evening I spent as a summer youth director at a church in a small town in North Dakota. Granted, it took nearly four years for her to understand what a catch I was; but I still believe God laid that groundwork and set us on that path that not only changed our lives but brought great joy and ministry as a result.

By recounting the story, by bringing it forward in a clear and faithful framework, we participate as the Israelites did in confessing not just the faith but our own faith experience and life. "*My* ancestor was a wandering Aramean" means that I am connected in a powerful and rich way with all of the stories that have gone before me; and connected with God, who has walked with me; and with my ancestors on that ongoing journey of faith and life.

What is the story that you would bring as a "first fruits" of the Lenten journey? How do you understand God's presence in your story?

HAVE FAITH, WILL TRAVEL
ROMANS 10:8b-13

The gas grill looked so nice on the box: big, shiny, ready to receive all of the culinary creations I could muster up. Coming as a birthday present in January in the Dakotas meant that I would have to do the assembly in the living room instead of on the back deck. I opened the box, expecting to see a couple of different pieces that needed to be put together. I did not expect to see the equivalent of an unassembled jumbo jetliner sitting inside the box! There were igniters and hoses and burners and tiny and large screws and many, many pieces that just had no right to be called part of a gas grill. I spread the pieces out all over the living room floor and picked up the assembly guide and felt fear. Actually, I came face to face with the possibility that I was not going to get this put together properly. Then I had the flashing image of a huge gas fireball shooting skywards with hotdogs and steaks close behind. Sure, I had the manual; but it would have been much nicer to have had someone I could trust to help me put it together.

That is the case with most everything we do. It is terribly difficult to write a completely accurate and usable instruction or teaching manual. Just imagine explaining on paper, either in script or with drawings, how to tie your shoes or how to do your taxes! How different it is to have a parent or a big sister or brother or a mentor to help walk us through the steps of those difficult things of life.

How much better it is as well to have someone along side of us to participate in the living of life itself, someone we could trust and rely on. With that person, we would not have to fear even when we make mistakes or errors in trying to build our lives up into good and near-perfect assemblages.

In Romans 10, Paul appears to be highly critical of the Law. The best he could say is in verse 2, where he stated, "I can testify that they have a zeal for God"; but he had to complete the sentence with "but it is not enlightened." Remember that Paul, also known as Saul, was a strong and faithful Jew, an adherent to the Law, "blameless before God" in keeping the law of Moses. However, in Chapter 10, he minced no words in explaining that the following of the Law is an effort to establish one's own righteousness apart from God; and the effort is ripe for failure. It is not a matter that the Law is bad or corrupt at all; it just appears to be something that no one can follow or keep completely all the time; and in that failure, one fails in attaining "righteousness," a word that means "a right or restored relationship with God." The Jews believed that the Law was the path to establishing that just relationship. Paul said that, at the end of the day, righteousness emerges from something more than obeying the Law.

It is similar to the situation I encountered when I was in New Orleans in February of 2006. I know the city pretty well, and I could identify most of the streets and main roadways as we drove through it. However, when we went into the 9th Ward, where incredible devastation had occurred with the break of levees and millions of gallons of water had destroyed blocks and blocks of neighborhoods, I would have been completely lost if I had been on my own with only a roadmap. The maps no longer made sense because life had literally been turned upside down. How comforting it was to have someone else in the driver's seat, someone who did not need a map, who knew the way through the worst areas, and who could bring us safely and surely out of that wilderness of collapsed houses and destruction.

In our faith as Christians, Paul said, we are invited to rely on Someone and not something to help us get through the journey of life. Even more, that Someone opens the door to the relationship with God that is full and complete, for we come to understand that God has been at work raising Christ from the dead and bringing us salvation. Our work as Christians is transformed from living a "good" life, obedient to the Law as a means of building our own innate righteousness to living a life that trusts in the work and actions of God through Christ. The journey becomes one of relying on Jesus as Lord. *Lord* means "one who is the master of a household." We belong to the household in which Jesus is in charge; and by that relationship, we have a relationship with God that is eternal and good.

As we take on the journey of Lent, that is, the journey of faith in our own lives, we go beyond a map and ride along with someone who knows the way clearly. Now, of course, this does not mean that we sit in the back seat and ignore all that is outside! I think an important part of being human is to be watchful and to participate in the journey. I believe humans are to live as fully as possible following honorable, ethical, and holy standards: living out of love, justice, hope, forgiveness, and honesty. That way of living, however, is not meant to serve as a path to our own righteousness. It is simply the way we have been created, and our lives will only make sense as we live as truly as possible to our created nature. In a simple word, Jesus Christ our Lord saves us so that we may live as fully human, created by a loving and just God to live out the same qualities in our existence. This is what living according to God's law is all about.

Paul says, "There is no distinction between Jew and Greek" (verse 12), that is, there is no difference between the natures of someone who follows the Law or someone who does not. The key is whether that person is willing to "call on the name of the Lord and be saved." Are you willing to trust the entire journey of your life to the guidance of God through Jesus Christ? Unfortunately, many of us chase after a roadmap, a law book, or an instruction manual to claim our own righteousness. In some areas of our church, the Christian faith is reduced to a code of "right living" in which we ask what Jesus would do and think that if we live that way we will somehow achieve our own salvation. We think that righteousness is a matter of being good, obedient, or lawful. Many of us, sadly enough, have transformed the life-saving, renewing relationship with the living Christ back into a series of dos and don'ts, believing God punishes and blesses us for what we do or do not do on the journey to heaven.

We need to return to Paul's important words in Romans 10.

We need to start over again with the realization that we simply cannot do enough good to establish our own place in eternal life and in righteousness. What we do is far second to God's saving power and grace in Jesus Christ. We are called to rely on God's power to set us free and to reclaim us through Christ. What we "do" is but a response of gratitude for what God, through Christ, has already done. Our actions reflect the reltionship and express the love and gratitude we have for Christ. As followers of Christ, we should never believe that our actions pave the way to heaven or make us more desirable to God. As verse 13 says, "Everyone who calls on the name of the Lord shall be saved."

The journey of Lent that we take, then, is a journey in which we realize and reclaim what God has already done for us and how powerful it is to rely on Someone else to direct that journey in the first place.

How is trusting Jesus Christ different from trying to live out a law as a path to righteousness? What connections do you see between trust in Christ and obedience to God's law?

CONFIRMATION CLASS
LUKE 4:1-13

Long after a conversation is over, have you ever come up with the perfect statement you would like to have made and wished you could go back in time? Often, the best we create on the spot is something like, "Oh yeah, well ..." Growing up with seven siblings, all of whom had heads that were rather "hard," discussions, debates, dialogues, and arguments were common. We would debate the primacy of vegetables (of course, corn is the best) or even what the true lyrics were on a song that no one could understand! Unfortunately, many of our "conversations" ended with someone using the phrase that was forbidden from our family language yet was still used with fear and trembling: "Shut up!" I suppose it was banned because the elders of the household grew tired of hearing it used over and over again; or maybe they believed that it was no one's right to silence the words of another, no matter how dumb or ignorant my brothers or sisters could be. When we said, "Shut up!" we knew we had crossed the line; the debate was done; and if it were in the hearing range of Mom or Dad, we would soon hear a lecture and stern warning that that phrase had no place in our family's discourse.

So pardon me as I read Luke 4, where the devil tempts Jesus in the wilderness, that I secretly wish Jesus would have just said, "Shut up!" At least it would sanctify some of my childhood conversations.

Luke offers fascinating imagery in this chapter. We read that Jesus was "full of the Holy Spirit" and that he was led by that same Spirit into the "wilderness" for "forty days." While in the wilderness, he was tempted by the devil. Luke enjoyed the phrase "full of the Spirit," for he used it in Acts to describe the disciples on Pentecost, the naming of the deacons, Stephen in his speech to the crowd, and Barnabas. A sense of power and resonance is found in these words; and it is appropriate that Jesus, following his baptism and the descending of the Spirit, should be well-filled with such a presence for his time of growth and testing. These 40 days (often known as a "perfect" number and used to designate our 40 days of Lent) appear to be, for all intent and purpose, the time of Jesus' "confirmation." He had been baptized, and now it was time for him to be tested and strengthened in the faith so he could answer honestly the questions of his own faith.

Confirmation best happens in the wilderness. That is, if we only test our beliefs and our faith in the midst of things that are known and normal, we may tend to give the easy answers and not touch the core of our soul in discovering what we believe and in whom we place our trust. Jesus' experience in the wilderness suggests the 40 years of wandering in the wilderness by his ancestors before they came to the Promised Land.

The words *testing* and *tempting* are used interchangeably, but they are not quite the same. The word *test* really comes from an ancient word for the vessel or cup in which someone would place a mineral to "test" or assay the metal through heating and fire. A test is a well-crafted experiment to see if something, or someone, is truly authentic. *Tempt* also includes aspects of testing, but it carries with it the possibility of failure. "Lead us not into temptation" is a prayer that God would keep us from being exposed to such a possibility of failure of faith and action. The time of testing for Jesus may have been set by God and the Holy Spirit, but the devil was busy "tempting" Jesus with the opportunity to fail. It was a dangerous time; and we should not so quickly assume that this was just something Jesus had to get through, like a 50-minute confirmation class on a Wednesday night. The experience in the wilderness called Jesus to make drastic life and death decisions about who he was and what he believed. It is not enough for him to tell the devil to "shut up." The temptations are those that are woven into the very fabric of our human experience; and Jesus overcame their normal, natural, dangerous natures.

The first definition of *famish* is "to die of hunger." Now, I have been hungry before; and it is not comfortable. I have, however, never been starving, nor, by this definition, "famished." We use those words as hyperboles to let our host know that we are hungry and eager to enjoy the meal. Jesus had gone a great length of time without eating, but wait! He is the Son of God and filled with the Spirit! Couldn't he have just re-created nature into something useful to sustain his life? Heavens, what harm would it have done to change one little piece of creation from a stone to a loaf of bread, especially when it would have saved his life? It is reasonable, rational, and even sensible, if we let ourselves think about it. However, this was a journey of faith, even for Jesus. Jesus knew that there is more to human need than satisfying one's hunger. A person lives through reliance upon God. Our true life is found beyond having our stomachs and needs met. Our life is found as we place it solely in the hands of God to sustain and keep us even when we would rather fix things ourselves with a little magic or manipulation.

The next test in the confirmation class is the temptation to hold on to power. Now, in one sense, it seems kind of silly for the devil to "give" the kingdoms to Jesus. Isn't Jesus already the Lord of all? Why did he need to get something from the devil that he already has? The temptation actually went deeper than that, especially for us. "I am in charge of my own life!" In fact, I deserve to be in charge of much more than that. If I only were the king of the world, the boss of all, think of how much better the world would be! Even more seductive: I just want a little power. I just want to be able to own "this much" or this thing or rule over this small

kingdom of my own—not everything. I just want to have some place on this earth or even some place in my own life where I am the ultimate authority. With that thought, I take back from God just a small part of my life; and I choose what is best for me instead of discerning what God would intend for me. It's not a big kingdom; but it might as well be, because the walls that surround my piece of self-reliance only serve to separate me from the God who deserves all of me, all of my worship, and all of my heart. "Worship the Lord your God, / and serve only him." Jesus answered the devil in a way that removed the possibility of receiving a kingdom from him; he chose to serve God.

The final temptation in this confirmation journey is perhaps the most insidious one. Jesus was transported up to the pinnacle of the Temple, which of course was the highest point; and with the Temple resting on a high hill, the altitude must have been dizzying. Again, Jesus was challenged by the devil: "If you are the Son of God ..." That part of our language—the "if"—is always a challenge to our integrity and a demand by others to prove ourselves, as though that is necessary. Yet, so often, we take that challenge just to prove to ourselves that we are right. The devil tempted Jesus to throw himself off the Temple as he quoted Scripture to Jesus about God's care and protection.

We all believe God will protect us, don't we? I know that the most difficult and heartbreaking experiences of my ministry have come when someone who was so loved and so prayed for still succumbed to either tragedy or death. "Why didn't God save her?" "Should we have prayed more?" "Doesn't God care for us the way we think?" It is so easy for a wedge to be driven into the relationship between an otherwise faithful person and God with this situation. Here, on top of the Temple, Jesus was asked to prove how much God loved him. If he jumped, God would have to save him, right? How could God let his own Son die?

We know the answer to that on Good Friday. It was death with a purpose and an eternal truth. This temptation is to turn God into our assistant, or our magic genie, who will protect us even when we act with arrogance or stupidity. For Jesus to jump off the Temple would mean he had already thrown off any respect, any understanding, and any humility in his relationship with God. What God would end up saving would be someone who had given up being the Son of God.

God promises salvation and the assurance that in life or death or life beyond death we will never be beyond God's presence and love. That makes jumping off of temples, literally or figuratively in our lives, just a waste of time. Indeed, there is no use in putting God to the test. God has already shown us how much we are loved through the death of the Son and through the Resurrection. Perhaps it is time for us to be finished with confirmation class and to continue on the journey of Lent with Jesus, understanding more clearly what it meant for Jesus to be that faithful, honest, and authentic Son. As we continue to journey with Jesus to Golgotha, we also strive to be a son or daughter of God.

How do the temptations of Jesus in Luke 4 speak to you about your journey of faith?

Something Greater to Come

Scriptures for Lent:
The Second Sunday

Genesis 15:1-12, 17-18
Philippians 3:17–4:1
Luke 13:31-35

As a child, I loved most of December because it seemed every event moved us closer to the magnificent celebration of Christmas. We baked Christmas goodies. We stood the tree in its honored corner of the living room. We opened the Sears toy catalog and made our lists. We watched Dad put the outside Christmas lights up, which was often agonized because he always seemed to wait for the coldest and windiest day to climb the ladder with the staple gun that never worked. We lit each candle of the Advent wreath and talked about its meaning. All of these events swept us toward Christmas with a sense of joy, anticipation, eagerness, and excitement.

In Lent, however, it has always been hard to "look eagerly" to Easter because in part it requires us to race to Good Friday and death. How could we anticipate such a joyful day without restraint when we saw that the path required us to walk straight through the struggles of Holy Week with its somber and reflective tones? Yet as we study this week's Scripture offerings, we find three remarkable illustrations of anticipation and hopeful waiting. We find God in the midst of the Bible verses, inviting us to take the far-sighted view, to lift up our heads, and go down the path of Lent, to appreciate and even cherish the promise that comes to us as people of faith.

START COUNTING
GENESIS 15:1-12, 17-18

Is it more difficult to keep a promise that you have made or to trust that a promise made to you will be kept? The first, of course, requires faithfulness and honesty: I will do what I said I would do. The second, however, requires faith or the willingness to be patient, hopeful, and waiting for something yet unrevealed to come to pass by the hand of another. Given my frequent inclination to take charge of things, I believe that receiving a promise is harder than keeping one. "Are you sure? When do think it will happen? Do you really have the power to do that? Did I hear you correctly? You're not just joking, are you?"

Abram traveled hundreds of miles. He and Sarai traveled with his father, Terah, from Ur to Haran where they settled. Then at God's command, Abram traveled through Canaan down to Egypt, because there was a famine in Canaan; back to the Negeb desert; and finally to Hebron in what would become the hill country of Judah generations later, about 20 miles from the site of Salem, the future Jerusalem. He left his home, his father, and all he knew to become a virtual nomad because God told him to do so. God's command, of course, carried with it two other promises: Abram would be the father of a great nation, and he would be a blessing to the world. These were God's promises, and Abram did his best to be patient and believe that God would do as God said.

In Genesis 15, however, we find a crack in Abram's faith. In Genesis 15:2-3, Abram complained that somehow God had not kept the holy promise of a family to arise from Abram. As we tend to do, Abram looked at things from a near-sighted, have-to-have-things-happen-now kind of approach. "You've given me no offspring!" spoken by a man who was approaching his nineties.

God's response to Abram carries the same power for us today as it did for Abram. God calmly answered Abram by reaffirming what was true even though it had not yet come to pass. A child, a son of Abram, would be born to carry on his lineage. Imagine yourself as Abram at this moment: God brings you outside of your home and into God's "house" and invites you to do some stargazing—actually, some starcounting. God wants you to count the stars if you can. Of course, if you have ever tried such a silly exercise on a moonless night out in the country, you know how utterly overwhelming the number of stars happens to be. God may be quiet for a few minutes, letting you consider the magnitude of the universe. Then imagine a whisper in your ear, the voice of God saying, "So shall your descendants be."

For Abram, it was a faith-restoring moment; and he once again trusted in the future held by God and in God's power and willingness to make that future happen.

God then added to the first covenant made with Abram in Genesis 12:1-3. In a ritual that is mysterious and ancient, God directed Abram to make a sacrifice of a number of different animals, laying them out on the ground, cut in two before God. After sunset, not only was a covenant of a great nation of descendants given to Abram but God also offered the land of Canaan and the land of many other nations into Abram's hand (12:18). Abram would cease being a nomad, a wanderer, and would instead find his home in the land of Canaan.

After studying this story today, the question for us is pretty simple yet profoundly deep. What has God promised you? First, we could ask what promises God has made to you that have already been realized. For some of us it is a promise of meaningful life's work, a home, children, or a good family. However, some of us may not have received those types of promises or are living without these things as part of our lives. Does that mean that God does not keep promises or does not make promises in the first place? Are holy promises today only reserved for a few? What do I trust in my life, and how can I know what to expect in my life with God? The important piece to all of this, I believe, is learning to recognize God's promises not yet come to pass. Even Abram got nervous and questioned the promise of a descendant to be brought by God. Think, however, of how far less dramatic promises we begin to question of God: I'm not as successful as I wanted to be. Why, God? My children are not what I hoped they would be. Why, God? I don't have the comforts of life that I wanted to have. Why, God? I'm lonely. Why, God?

Too often we turn our wants in life into things we think God should have promised to us; or we turn our needs into frustrations that God has not taken care of things. We are impatient; and in that impatience, we tend to forget the life-promise and forget how to wait with anticipation and hope. We forget that the fulfillment of God's promises to us may mean waiting a long time. One thing is certain, however. God's first and central promise to us never changes, as it never changed for Abram: God will never leave us alone in life. God has promised to be with us wherever we go, even if we end up far away from where we should be. God's love and grace is never beyond our reach. It is only we who decide not to reach for those promises fulfilled. When those times come in our lives, when doubt and even hopelessness or frustration in life seem to reign, perhaps the most appropriate thing to do would be to stand outside on a clear night and count the stars and recall once again God's promises yet to unfold. Remember that God promises something greater to come and God's presence is never apart from us.

How do you understand God's promises? What has God promised you? For what do you wait with anticipation to see God working out in your life and in your world?

CITIZENS OF A HEAVENLY REALM
PHILIPPIANS 3:17–4:1

I have had my picture on three different passports in my life. The pictures in the last two show the progression of age, I am afraid; but they also contain wonderful memories of travel wrapped up in visa stamps carelessly applied on blank pages in the book. The first passport picture, however, is a bit different. In the early 1960s, our family moved to Australia for two years—a family with a mother, a father, and, at that time, six children, ranging in ages from nine to not-quite-one. My father, in the military, had his official passport; and for some reason, my mother and all six children were pictured on the second passport. (I always wondered how they would identify my baby sister Julie at nine months!) The funniest thing about the picture, however, is that apparently they must have told us all not to smile, because the black and white picture shows a gaggle of children with their chins pulled down to their necks, their mouths turned into artificial frowns, as we all must have done our best to portray the seriousness of a United States passport. We looked like an entire family in serious need of jaw and dental work. Whenever I have used a passport, I have always felt a sense of place and protection. The United States knows me. See my passport? I am a citizen of that country, and I am under that country's security; and I have a place there. What a great feeling to belong somewhere and to claim that place as my own.

As Paul wrote to the church at Philippi in Macedonia, he was writing to perhaps his most beloved congregation. The letter is filled with more tenderness and encouragement than nearly any other letter in the New Testament. Paul wanted the Philippians to speak, think, act, live, hope, and dream as beloved followers of Christ, seeking and imitating the best way to live as faithful people. In 3:17, Paul used himself as the example they should follow. This sounds rather arrogant and not something we would think to write in a pastoral letter. However, remember that the early church, especially outside of the Jewish Christian congregations, would have no writings, no traditions, and no code of behavior or discipline to follow such as we have in the New Testament and in 2,000 years of Christian tradition. All the Philippians had was Paul as he came, lived among them, brought them to Christ, and established the congregation. "Imitate me" must have been spoken with tremendous humility. Paul communicated his own continual striving to live out God's heavenly call in 3:12-14.

The city of Philippi was located in Macedonia on the Via Egnatia, an important route from Byzantium in the east to the Adriatic Sea. The citizens of the city enjoyed the privileges of Roman citizenship. People who lived there practiced a variety of religions, including the official cult of the Roman emperor.[1] The way of Christ was a different path than the paths offered by existing religions. Paul offered them a new image in verse 20: "But our citizenship is in heaven, and it is from there that we are expecting a Savior, the Lord Jesus Christ." In other words, in contrast to the citizenship of Rome, the people who follow Jesus have a different citizenship and, therefore, a different way of living. They are called to something much greater, something holy and loving, a "heavenly realm." As citizens of heaven, they were to live in expectation of the coming of the Lord Jesus Christ. The use of the word *savior* was also used to refer to the emperor and to the various Hellenistic gods.[2] That "something to look forward to" must have encouraged the Philippians to lift their eyes beyond earthly examples of living to heaven and to find a new and a different way to act, react, and exist.

Paul spoke words of transformation. What was to come would be far different than what is. Even our human bodies would be transformed and "conformed" to Christ's glorious body (verse 21). In a real sense, those who read and heard Paul's letter were to gather up the future possibility and hope and bring it into the present, seeing something coming to pass that is far greater than Rome and all of its power. Paul offered them a vision of the future and encouraged them to "stand firm in the Lord" (4:1).

What incredibly difficult work it is to reform action to match a future hope! Yet Paul's words to the church at Philippi set a standard for our trust and our behavior as well. The Christian faith is not merely a set of moral principles to follow. It is not a rule book of good behavior. When we carelessly or unthinkingly diminish the power of the gospel to a book of manners or ethical actions, we forget what Paul was saying to the Philippians. What he says to us in this Scripture is that our citizenship belongs to another realm.

As citizens of heaven, we have a different outlook, a different mindset, a transformed being, because we know that our greatest hope lies in the expectation of our Savior Jesus Christ's presence with us. Our actions and our behavior naturally should proceed from our understanding of who we are rather than from a list of dos and don'ts. Such a list often undergirds a fear: "If I am not good, I won't go to heaven." When I choose to see myself as a citizen of heaven, brought into that relationship through Jesus Christ, my focus and orientation moves from acting like everyone else acts to acting as a transformed citizen of heaven, conformed in a marvelous way to Christ's glory. It is in this holy citizenship that we find a truly authentic and joyful existence. In this heavenly citizenship, we re-present Christ to the world; and we re-present a heavenly way of living—at least we should; and we can, if we choose to do so. It is then that our choice of behavior calls us to reflect our citizenship instead of "when in Rome, act like the Romans." Christ calls us to live differently, not as a rulebook of behavior but as a response to a life transformed by Christ.

What does it mean to you to live as a citizen of heaven? How might you grow new behaviors and leave behind those actions that are not "heavenly"? What would it mean for you to live anticipating a transformed life by the power of Christ?

WAIT UNTIL THE TIME COMES
LUKE 13:31-35

Anxious inaction often takes more effort than acting immediately. Watch a dog that has been told to "stay" stare at a doggy treat in front of him and wait for his trainer to say, "Ok!" Watch a basketball player who has been told to get ready to go in as a substitute during a game. The non-action may well require more work than the act itself. It has been said that patience is power because it holds the reins of any act.

Isn't it odd in today's Scripture from Luke that the Pharisees appear to be trying to save Jesus? Normally we think of the Pharisees and Jesus locked in a battle with each other over religious and political authority. Granted, it could be that the Pharisees were only trying to scare Jesus into leaving the area; but it is also possible that even with the great criticism that Jesus levied

against the Pharisees that some of them were more on Jesus' side than Herod's. If Herod were breathing threats against a holy teacher of Israel, perhaps some of the Pharisees would also be in danger. Whatever the case, Jesus responded to the news of a threat against his life with almost a sense of bravado: "Go and tell that fox for me" (verse 32). To refer to Herod as a fox was an insult. The animal metaphor variously suggests craftiness, lack of strength, and voracious destruction.[3]

Jesus used the opportunity to announce that the actions to come, that were to be part of the difficult struggle of Holy Week, were going to happen by Jesus' calendar and Jesus' decision. Herod was going to have to wait. No one was going to kill Jesus until Jesus decided it was time.

I like this Scripture because it reveals the power of Jesus Christ, one who was far greater than the religious and political authorities of his time. Let's look at Jesus' plans and his patience. Jesus stated that he had work still to be done: the casting out of demons and the curing of the sick (verse 32). Both of those were natural expressions of his power over the universe and even over evil itself. It is as if Jesus said, "I'm too busy for you to kill me, Herod. My schedule is booked for now in expressing the power of God to this world. You'll have to take a seat, and I might get to you later." He trivialized a king, and his words convey his own inner greatness.

We can sense Jesus' understanding of timing in his speech, and he was careful to give the impression that the actions that would change the world would be coming soon but "not today" and not tomorrow. "On the third day I finish my work" (verse 32). Jesus communicates a sense of clarity about timing. It is God's timing, not Herod's.

I have always loved those kinds of movies where the hero is beset by all sorts of evil and harmful enemies; and just when it looks as though there is no hope, no way of escape, no way to combat the overwhelming actions of the evil ones, the hero reveals power that has been there all along. The right moment has come, and victory over evil is utter and complete. I cannot help cheering every time it happens. I believe that God's power will ultimately defeat evil in the world. Evil will not and cannot ultimately withstand the power of God. Often we have the sense that evil is winning, that God has either decided not to be involved or that God is weakened somehow. Sometimes in our own lives, we have a sense that our battles are being lost against much stronger powers. We wonder if we will ever be able to withstand all that is being thrown against us. Someone we love is caught in a deadly illness. A child is hurt. Injustice seems to be ruling. We are trapped in a pervasive loneliness, depression, or fear. At such times, it is important for us to see Jesus' words in Luke 13:31-34 as words of hope. It is important for us to find strength and power in waiting. When the timing is right, God's loving power will once again prove that nothing can separate us from that holy love. We just need to wait.

Jesus lamented Jerusalem at least twice in the Gospel of Luke. In 13:34-35 and again in 19:41-44, he mourned and wept over the lost promise of the city. *Jerusalem* means "house of peace," and yet it was in Jerusalem that often prophets came to their deaths as they tried to bring change and reform. Jesus seemed to know at that time that his future would be found in Jerusalem. He longed to bring true peace to the city, to free it from turmoil and intrigue. In the end, Jesus had to say, "Your house is left to you" (13:35). You are alone.

Jesus was fond of quoting Scripture as a way of tying his own actions to that of prophecy and tradition. "Blessed is the one who comes in the name of the LORD" (Psalm 118:26). A similar phrase is also quoted as Jesus entered Jerusalem (Luke 19:38). The Psalm reference is a processional psalm of thanksgiving for the rescuing of a king or an individual from danger in battle. It celebrates God as the source of strength, loyalty, and salvation.

Jesus said to all those who sought to silence him or to remove him from the scene, "Not yet." Jesus did not react to their threats out of fear or anger. He did not adjust his work or ministry because he thought he was in danger. Instead, he moved forward on the path that eventually did take him to Jerusalem, through the gates in a parade with cheers; and then it was on to the cross, the grave, and resurrection. All of the events were set by God's timetable, and it was a matter of waiting for the right time to come. It would not be hurried. It is that "time" that in Greek is known as *kairos*, the perfect moment in which something should happen, instead of *chronos*, which is the time you would find on a watch or a calendar. God's *kairos* is found in today's story as all the players, and we too, wait for something great to come that will change and heal the world.

All the examples of waiting, anticipating, and preparing that we found in today's readings reflect the time that God intends and sets for our lives. We ask a faithful, discerning question when we ask, "Is this the right time, God, for me to act this way? Does this time fit with your time and your will for my life and my world?" Instead of asking for God to hurry up and make something happen for us right now, we are called to anticipate and trust God's time. We are called to wait, to pray, and to be ready to respond. When we have honestly discerned how God is calling us to live, we will be able to move ahead doing what we do as a faithful response to God. We resist the temptation to react and "do something" because we lack the patience to wait upon God. What a better approach to life! How much more gracious and responsive we can be as Christ's followers when we take on this important discipline during this Lenten season.

How would practicing the spiritual discipline of waiting for and discerning God's timing affect your interactions with others in your life? How might you involve others in this habit of reflection and discernment, whether in your family, your work, or your church or community?

From *The New Interpreter's Bible*, Vol. XI (Abingdon Press, 1994); pages 470-71.
[2] From the footnote for Philippians 3:20-21 in *The New Interpreter's Study Bible*; page 2105.
[3] From the footnote for Luke 13:32 in *The New Interpreter's Study Bible*; page 1881.

Moving to Repentance

Scriptures for Lent: The Third Sunday
Isaiah 55:1-9
1 Corinthians 10:1-13
Luke 13:1-9

I was not a terribly rebellious teenager. OK, a little bit; but it involved long hair and girlfriends and curfews more than things illegal, immoral, or dangerous. Frankly, I could not figure out why my parents did not simply give me everything I wanted and then stay out of my way so I could do what I wanted. I was pretty independent—except for the car, the clothes, the money, the food, the house, and just about everything else that made up my life.

I went away to college and seminary and got married and had sons of my own; and it did not take long to recognize just how much my parents had loved me. They cared for me and tolerated me through times when my behavior and attitudes were unlovable—not terrible but unlovable. Over the course of time, I quietly and surely repented of the past. I discovered my deep respect for my parents.

Perhaps the most important work of any human being is repentance. The word *repent* means "to turn around, to re-assess, to come to a different understanding." It is to reclaim a relationship with God that leads to living life God's way. We respond to the world as one who more closely reflects the love and presence of God.

Scriptures for the third Sunday of Lent deal with repentance. They will guide us on our spiritual journey with Jesus to Golgotha to reclaim the new life we discover as we turn again to God.

PROMISE
ISAIAH 55:1-9

A good friend of mine was my roommate for two years in seminary. Daniel was from Liberia; and I recall his first days in America in Dallas, Texas. He needed items from a variety of stores, so I drove him to a mall. Living in a Western consumer culture for my whole life, I was not quite prepared for the look on Daniel's face when we first started walking through the stores. They were packed with everything you would ever want and much of what you did not need. He was in shock. As we rode escalators and saw floor after floor of merchandise, he began to say things such as "Wow"; "This is like paradise, man"; "I can't even believe this exists"; and "This is simply unbelievable." It was fun to point out particularly "unbelievable" items and watch his reaction. I imagine my reaction would be similar to his if I were to visit his country and view its natural beauty. When we are invited to see and experience something we never believed existed before, our reaction may be similar to Daniel's.

Imagine being hungry and thirsty and having someone open the doors of a banquet hall and say, "Come on in! Enjoy! Eat and drink to your heart's delight, and there will be no bill!" Our response should be, "Wow! That's unbelievable! This is paradise!" All that you ever desired to enjoy at a feast is set before you, and someone else is covering the cost. All you have to do is to eat and enjoy.

The prophet Isaiah wrote the words of Chapter 55 in order to give the people of Israel an image of what it means to live under God's covenant of peace and grace. The nation would soon be restored after its time of captivity in Babylon. Isaiah went further than the promise of being allowed to return to their homeland. He offered a vision of the people returning to God and reclaiming the vital and life-giving relationship that identified them as a people. The feast was more than a feast of food and drink. The image of the meal communicated the richness and satisfaction found in reclaiming the covenant relationship with God. Repentance, turning again to God, would guide them to a feast of love, acceptance, and true life. However, it required a response. The promise was offered. Now, what would the people of Israel do? "Seek the LORD, while he may be found, call upon him while he is near" (verse 6).

We often use verse 7 to call us into prayer; but in Chapter 55, it was meant to call the people to return to the covenant relationship with God. "Let the wicked forsake their way, and the unrighteous their thoughts." This verse talks about far more than changing the ways a person acts. The Hebrew word translated to "wicked" refers to one who is guilty of a crime, guilty of a sin against God or another human, and hostile toward God. The word translated "unrighteous" echoes the word *wicked*. It suggests trouble, sorrow, idolatry, and wickedness. The sense of being separated from God is common to both words.

We often applaud independent, self-sufficient persons; but when it comes to our relationship with God, self-sufficiency can create a wall that separates us from God. Wicked or unrighteous people, in the biblical sense, forget that they need God. They assume that they can live their lives, make their decisions, and create their own world apart from the God who gives them breath. (*Wickedness* and *unrighteousness* describe an orientation of one's life more than behaviors, an orientation that ignores God's presence and covenant gift.)

Isaiah 55 says, in effect, let the ones who think they are doing just fine on their own, apart from God, once again repent and turn back into a relationship with God. "Let them return to the LORD, that he may have mercy on them, / and to our God, for he will abundantly pardon" (verse 7). Isaiah called the people to return to the covenant with God, who is greater than they could imagine and whose thoughts were above their thoughts. This was the call by the prophet to the people to come home to the covenant relationship that would identify the people of Israel.

So, when we think of the word *wicked* as pointing to our separateness from God, how wicked might we be? Have we heard the promise of the feast of life and covenant from God? Do we remain outside of the banquet hall, hungry and thirsty for something that satisfies and reluctant to give up control over our own lives? It is an easy pattern of life to slip into. We become successful over a number of different areas of life. We amass property and wealth. We have good relationships with our family. We are respected by those with whom we work. We are tempted to say, "I'm doing just fine all by myself." The truth is we are doing wickedly fine the moment we think we can get by without God.

How differently would it look to enter that banquet hall fully in our lives, to repent, to accept and live out the promise that God offers to us? Imagine the fullest sense of humility, gratitude, and openness to receiving a gift. Imagine yourself as one who stands in continual need of the grace of God in your life, which, of course, is exactly our position as human beings. God's grace begins with a promise, moves to a call to repent, and offers the invitation to new life for all who would turn and follow. It was true for the nation of Israel, and it is true for us.

What exists in your life right now that might lead you into wickedness, into thinking that your life is fine without God's grace? How might repentance lead you to a renewed relationship with God?

WARNING
1 CORINTHIANS 10:1-13

I have a small chip on my right front tooth. I have had the chip since I was about nine years old. I had spent most of the afternoon leaping from the ground to the top of the mailbox in front of our house, and I was actually getting some pretty great height and spring to it. I would leap, climb the rest of the way, and then push myself off and away to land on the ground like a gymnast. At the time, I thought it was a good skill that most every young boy should learn.

After spending hours in that pursuit of excellence, it happened that my mother and various brothers and sisters were outside by the mailbox. I thought it was time to show my stuff. I said, "Watch!" As I leapt with grace and aplomb to the top of the mailbox, my mother shouted, "Be Careful! You need to watch what you are doing!"

What possible use would her warning be in this endeavor? I smiled broadly and pushed off from the mailbox for my dismount. Muscle fatigue from the hours of exercise, sweaty palms, and the need to show off to my siblings made me miscalculate ever so slightly the push away from the box. I still can recall the sensation of biting into bent steel, landing on my knees on the ground, and feeling a strong tingling sensation in my tooth. The mailbox was now the proud owner of about 1/16 of an inch of enamel. The tooth was fine, just a bit shorter than its neighbor. Fortunately, I broke nothing other than my tooth. The worst sensation came when I looked in my mother's eyes. She did not say a thing. She took me in the house and had me suck on a lukewarm washcloth.

In 1 Corinthians 10:1, Paul writes, "I do not want you to be unaware!" He invited the church at Corinth to remember the faith history of the Exodus in order to be vigilant about their living. Corinth was a Greek city, and it is likely that most of those to whom he addressed the letter were not from a Jewish background. Yet Paul claimed this as part of the faith history of the new Christians. He used the stories of the Exodus as a warning for those who would follow God. He reminded them that even though the ancestors shared the experience of the cloud, passing through the sea, eating spiritual food, drinking water from the rock, "God was not pleased with most of them, and they were struck down in the wilderness" (verse 5). They partook of all the elements of care and safety that God provided, but their faithfulness and devotion to God was weak. They did not survive the wilderness.

"Watch out! Be Careful!" Paul presented the stories to the Corinthians "as examples for us, so that we might not desire evil as they did" (verse 6). He told them to avoid idolatry, sexual immorality, testing God, and complaining (verses 7-10). Exodus 32:1-6 tells the story of the worship of the golden calf when Moses was on the mountain. Numbers 25:1-9 tells of the story that Paul related of how the children of Israel devoted themselves in the land of Moab to the worship of Ba'al and became sexually immoral. As a result, a plague came upon the people; and 24,000 died. Exodus 17 records the story of water from the rock. The people doubted God's provision. Moses "called the place Massah and Meribah, because the Israelites quarreled and tested the LORD, saying, 'Is the LORD among us or not?'" (Exodus 17:7). Exodus 16 recounts the complaining of the people in the wilderness: "The whole congregation of the Israelites complained against Moses and Aaron in the wilderness" (verse 2). All these examples illustrated the people's lack of faith and devotion to God.

What were the Corinthians to do with such examples of faithlessness before God? Was God to be viewed as a vengeful, raging, and angry deity? Paul reminded them of the Exodus in order to call them to vigilance and self-examination. If the Corinthians professed their faith and loyalty to God but at the same time indulged their own selfish, immoral, and anti-God desires, God would have no patience with them. Paul repeated 1 Corinthians 10:6 in verse 11: "These things happened to them to serve as an example, and they were written down to instruct us." Notice that Paul made sure to include himself in the need to "watch out." Verse 12 is the perfect watchful verse: "So if you think you are standing, watch out that you do not fall."

How were the Corinthians to do what was commanded of them and not succumb to acts that would bring their destruction? Paul gave them comfort, assurance, and one of the more interesting promises that we find in the New Testament: "God is faithful, and he will not let you be tested beyond your strength" (verse 13). Often, this verse is taken out of context to comfort those who are going through tough times in their lives, such as in illness, or death, or some other tragic situation. We hear over and over again how God will not give you something that tests you beyond what you can handle. This use of the verse suggests that God's plan for the faithful is to bring them such tragedy and pain that they almost give up their faith. Notice, though, as we study the Scripture, that this is not the meaning of this verse. The issue is temptation, not tragedy. We need to include the portion of the verse that precedes it and the portion that follows to understand Paul's statement.

First, Paul stated that we should watch out and not be too confident in our ability to live a holy life apart from God's grace. Second, Paul said that whatever testing we may endure, whatever experience that comes that may invite us to act in an immoral or idolatrous way, is nothing new. The temptation to an immoral life is common. Then, Paul offered the often-quoted verse that God is faithful (even when we often are not) and knows the strength of our ability to withstand temptation. It is not about enduring pain and tragedy. God knows our hearts, our strength of commitment, and our faith. As long as we remain within a relationship with God, God will not let something come that destroys that faith and commitment. As these common temptations or tests come to us, God will use those very temptations to show us how to endure and overcome them and thus remain strong in the relationship that God provides in Jesus Christ.

Can we hear the word of grace that is meant for us as well as the Corinthians? Do we realize the promise of God's sustaining care even when our hearts and minds might want to turn away? First Corinthians 10:1-13 points to repentance. The passage offers a warning in order to help the Corinthians and to help us as we read it centuries later, to turn to God rather than to our own inclinations. As we repent day by day, continually turning toward God and adjusting our focus on God's way, God will indeed help us find the way out of any situation that might otherwise lead us to live or to act as one who has not received the grace of Jesus Christ.

Where in your life right now, or recently, have you found yourself faced with the temptation to step away from the life-giving and loving relationship God offers? What might you do to turn again to the God who sustains you through temptations?

REPENT
LUKE 13:1-9

I can barely stand to watch television news programs. I am not a Pollyanna, and I do not need to have everything in this world painted with happy hues; but, frankly, watching the news exhausts and depresses me. I am not talking about acquiring the knowledge of what is happening in the world, in our nation, and in our communities. Such information keeps us linked with the world. I am talking about the sensational news such as the minute-by-minute investigation of a murder thousands of miles away, a tragedy of a family or of a child on the other side of the world, or other issues of pain that simply are beyond my control but well within our hearts to agonize over. We know more about a celebrity's murder case than we do our own grandparents' lives.

Because much of the news is live action, it grabs the attention of the part of our brain that is different than the part used for reading. It captures us and feeds our senses with fear, anxiety, and a sense of helplessness and despair. The anchor may end the broadcast with "And, finally, on a good note ...," but the previous 28 minutes are simply not healthy for me. I question whether they are for anyone else. How much of what we see on the news is necessary in order to be a caring person? How much adds to the disease of our society and world? How much is sensational exploitation of the despair of others? Such news leaves me with the sense that there is no resolution, no hope, and certainly no opportunity to create change. In the Christian life, the act that addresses such helplessness is repentance or turning to God and receiving the power to live God's way.

Luke 13 begins with a news report that generated questions and teachable moments for Jesus. People came to Jesus and talked about a recent tragedy. Pilate killed Galilean pilgrims who had gone to Jerusalem carrying sacrifices in order to worship in the Temple. Galilee was an area rife with insurrection and rebellion against Rome. Apparently, Pilate heard of their arrival and arranged for them to be murdered right in the Temple, the holiest of places. Their blood was mixed with their own offerings to God. Try to imagine the drama and horror of the murder. According to traditional Jewish belief, if someone endured a painful tragedy, it was a sign of God's judgment. Those who told the story probably were implying that the Galileans deserved their horrible death.

At this point, we once again are confronted with Jesus, who turned the beliefs and reasoning of the society upside-down. Jesus challenged their conclusion that the Galileans were worse sinners than others with a warning: "No, I tell you; but unless you repent, you will all perish as they did" (verse 3). Jesus' response contains good news and an urgent message about repentance. If a tragedy comes to you, it does not mean God was out to get you. He emphasized his point with another story of people who were killed by the falling tower of Siloam. He asked, "Do you think that they were worse offenders than all the others living in Jerusalem?" (verse 4). Jesus made it clear that tragedy in life does not imply a punishment for our misdeeds or evil life. It just happens, and God does not use horrible events such as September 11, tsunamis, hurricanes, or the death of a loved one to punish wrongdoing. There may be times when evil creates pain, but all pain is not the result of God's punishment of evil.

However, Jesus quickly turns the conversation into a strong and clear warning and call to everyone who listens: "No, I tell you; but unless you repent, you will all perish just as they did" (verse 5). Jesus did not mean that his listeners would also be killed in the Temple or have a tower crash on them. He meant that just as surely as those persons were dead, so anyone who would not repent would die. Now is the time to turn to God. Now is the time to receive life instead of a living death. Now is the time through repentance to find our life in God.

Jesus ended this conversation with a parable about a fig tree. The fig tree, old enough to bear fruit, was barren. So the man who owned the vineyard told the gardener to chop it down. The good news is that the gardener offered a different plan. Leave it be for just a while more, and let it be nourished and cared for; it may bear fruit next year. If not, then cut it down. The story says to me that hope exists in the midst of judgment. God is patient. God intends for us all to receive the word of good news, to be able to respond to the love and care God offers, and to respond with the fruit of repentance. God cares for us and will tend to us, but now is the time to give away a barren and empty existence and to find our life in Christ.

How do you understand repentance? If you are already a follower of Christ, how can repentance give meaning to your life of faith?

Reconciliation and New Beginnings

Scriptures for Lent:
The Fourth Sunday
Joshua 5:9-12
2 Corinthians 5:16-21
Luke 15:1-3, 11b-32

I knew I was in trouble when one lovely Sunday morning the bishop and his wife dropped in for worship at the church I was serving. Such a visit had never happened in my clergy life! It was disconcerting. I knew that something was in the works when the bishop invited me to have breakfast with him the following week. The number and types of questions he asked me led me to believe that the church I had been serving comfortably and enthusiastically for six years soon might not be my church.

Sure enough, about a week later, a superintendent from the Black Hills called me and offered me the incredible opportunity to serve a church three times larger and in need of some reconciliation and peace. Black Hills is about as far away as you can get from the Red River Valley, where I had lived for 25 years. I am a good United Methodist pastor, so I said yes. Through the new appointment, God led me to a wonderful new chapter in my life—a new beginning for so many things. My family had shared in six years of completely different scenes, experiences, joys, sadnesses, and life.

Perhaps you have known similar changes in your life. The question would be for you as it was for us. Should we move and uproot everything that is comfortable for us? Why upset a familiar routine? Moving would upset that way of life. However, when we were offered a new calling in our lives, a new way of living, or a new challenge, it was wise to be thoughtful about our response. God is a God of newness: new worlds, new invitations, new opportunities, and new life. This week's Scriptures invite us to think about newness and also about re-creating and reconciliation that can and should occur in our world today. Read the Scriptures from the standpoint of possibility and a new world very well may open to you.

A NEW LAND
JOSHUA 5:9-12

We lived in the Red River Valley of North Dakota for a quarter century. The dark brown soil in that region is perhaps the most fertile in the world. Eons ago it was under the waters of prehistoric Lake Agassiz. Bumper crops of all sorts were normal fare; and the rich, fertile land created a sense of peace for the people of North Dakota. There were only two drawbacks from declaring it paradise: bitter winters and mosquitoes. Fifty degrees below zero wind chills and mosquitoes the size of small birds meant that you spent your time either shivering or slapping, but it was home!

When we moved to the Black Hills, we officially stayed within the bounds of the Dakotas; but, frankly, we might as well have been in a foreign country. The sun quickly went down behind the hills, instead of spending hours slowly dropping beneath the distant horizon. The only crop was hay for the livestock, and most of the land was prairie. Everything rolled downhill. However, the Hills also held two marvelous surprises: warm winters and no mosquitoes. In the winter, the temperatures would reach into the 70s in January. As for the mosquitoes, you could actually walk outside on a summer evening and not feel your life's blood draining from you or hear the sound of a million buzzing bugs in your ear! Warm winters and no mosquitoes made it feel like a promised land. It was wonderful, but we still missed the Red River Valley.

When we first read Joshua 5, it sounds like a great celebration. The entire nation of Israel had crossed over the Jordan River on dry land just as they had crossed the Red Sea to freedom. They had purified themselves, and all males once again were circumcised as a sign of the covenant with God. Finally, they celebrated the ritual meal of Passover where they remembered that God brought them out of Egypt and 400 years of slavery, through the sea, through the wilderness. Now they were in the Promised Land. What a powerful and rich event for the people of Israel!

The next morning, however, as they awoke in the Promised Land after the Passover celebration, the people of Israel "ate the produce of the land, unleavened cakes and parched grain" (verse 11). The manna from heaven stopped. The change in food marked the transition from the wilderness wanderings to a life in the Promised Land.

What was it like to be without manna? Scripture does not tell us. However, the experience must have been unsettling to them. One thing consistent in the wilderness was the gathering and eating of the manna, just enough for the day (Exodus 16; Numbers 11:4-9). Now the manna was gone.

Everywhere they looked, none existed except for the one piece that had been preserved in the Holy of Holies beside the ark of the covenant as a witness to God's provision (Exodus 16:33-34). The Passover meal had been the celebration of new life, but what did it mean that there was no manna?

As important as the manna was for their lives in the wilderness where no crops were planted, in the land of Abraham the people could eat the food of Canaan; and they would be sustained by God's hand in a new way. Again, their days of wandering and living as nomads were over. God had brought them to the land flowing with milk and honey, and they would have grain and all sorts of sacred and blessed food that would become part of their way of life. Still, I wonder if sometimes, in a holy moment of celebration, the priest might not have opened the ark and shown the remaining piece of manna to the people; and those who could remember, would remember the days before Canaan and God's gracious gift to them.

Moving into the new land of Canaan meant a new life for every Israelite. Sharing the Passover meant linking the promise of the past with the promise of God's protection and care for the future. No longer having the manna as their sustenance meant a new way of thinking for the Israelites. It meant reconciling where and who they were in the wilderness with where and who they were after crossing the Jordan River. They needed to be reconciled with the promise of the Promised Land, given so many centuries ago, to Abraham and then to Jacob, who became Israel.

Imagine your ancestors leaving your home in 1507; and this year, 2007, you have come back to claim it as your own. It would seem foreign, strange, and unknown. I am sure it took time for the Israelites to be reconciled with the idea that they were no longer going to wander. They had been doing that for as long as many of them had been alive. It would have taken an effort to adjust to a new reality no matter how wonderful and blessed it might feel. Again, it was similar in one way to the sense my family had as we moved to the Hills. Everyone would ask us, "Don't you just love it here?" We did, but it was different from how we had lived for many years; and honestly, we had to get used to loving it.

Think about a time in your own life, either recently or long ago, when you were invited or led into a new and different experience and opportunity. Do you remember the excitement and the enthusiasm at the beginning and the willingness to move ahead? Do you remember catching yourself saying something such as, "This sure is different from what I knew before." Do you recall appreciating the new as you remembered the old?

For the Israelites, the time in the wilderness would be seen forever in their faith history as a holy and formative time. It was during this time of wandering that they were shaped into God's people. How different it would have been for them to leave Egypt and five days later be in Canaan! They entered the Promised Land as a different people, gathering up all the corporate memory of the wilderness time. It required a reconciliation of the past with the present and with the ever-emerging future. It required trust that all time is in God's hands.

When have you experienced a "new land"? Do you have a transition coming in your life that will require a great change and a shift in your mind and heart? How do you understand God's care and provision in a "new land" experience?

A NEW CREATION
2 CORINTHIANS 5:16-21

I love collecting stoneware crocks. It has been fun over the years, scouring back rooms of antique stores and rummage sales, looking for the special find. One time, early in my stoneware career, I found a small crock that was plain ugly. It was only two gallons, and someone had years before used it as a container for who knows what. The inside of the crock was covered in a concrete-like mess, which dribbled down the outside. It really was fairly worthless as a display item. For some reason, however, probably because the price was right, I bought it, took it home, and tried to see if I could renovate it, to reconcile it with my understanding of what a crock should look like.

The first soaking in hot water made no difference to its ugliness. I tried a little baking soda and some mild detergent. Again, it appeared to make no difference. Just when I thought I had wasted my money, I took a small knife and started to chip at the mess that appeared frozen on the crock. As I chipped, the mess started to loosen, chip off, and crumble before my eyes. After about 20 minutes of chipping, what had been an ugly piece of pottery was transformed into a pretty crock with a shiny, nearly perfect inside. It had been protected for years from the elements. As a bonus, the bottom of the crock had a special mark that made it even more valuable. It holds a special place in our collection, partly because of its innate value and partly because I no longer regard it as a waste of money. It is a treasure.

How do we look at the world, at each other, and at ourselves? As Paul wrote to the Corinthians, he made use of the word *eido*, which is translated "regard" in the New Revised Standard Version of the Bible. It is a great word because it means more than seeing with the eyes. It means "to perceive with the eyes and senses, to discover, to discern, to know, and to determine action that follows such knowing."

Paul said, "From now on, therefore, we regard no one from a human point of view; even though we once knew Christ from a human point of view, we know him no longer in that way" (verse 16). If nothing else in the Christian faith and the Christian community, this perspective of life—the willingness to see, know, and interact with persons as more than "plain old humans"—expresses the way in which God cherishes each of us as a special creation and loved child. From a human point of view, Paul saw the followers of Jesus as troublemakers for the Romans and the religious leadership of Israel. He would have understood Jesus as a threat. Jesus' death would have been a natural consequence of his own actions of standing against the establishment of Israel during a tumultuous time in its history.

Paul thought at one time that he should have been put to death, as should others who would stand against the Jewish and Roman authorities. No longer, however. He wrote about a new set of lenses in which to view the life, death, and resurrection of Jesus. This new way of seeing manifests as a willingness to see and claim what through normal eyes cannot be seen nor claimed. If anyone is in Christ, all is new.

Paul's use of the phrase "new creation" is resurrection talk. Just as Jesus Christ, on resurrection morning, did not simply wake up from the dead but was brought into a new being and a new existence by God's power, so we are brought into a new being, a new creation, where the old way of acting, talking, perceiving, and believing is transformed. The Christian faith is far more than learning how to live a good and moral life. It is far more than being consistent in going to church and loving our neighbors and praying to God. These ways of life are an expression of something much more profound. In Christ, we are brought into a new creation.

As we trust in Christ's redeeming power and love and in God's desire to reconcile us to God through Christ, we begin to live our lives within the realm of the eternal. Certainly, we are still living in the world; but we no longer view it as the way the rest of the world sees it. What once was our perspective and approach to life has been transformed. No longer is our focus upon making sure that our needs and our particular wants are fulfilled. Now we give all that we are for God's use. We share the message of reconciliation with God. We seek to live in Christ—forever new, forever touching eternal things such as limitless love; pure forgiveness; and an honest, open offering of ourselves for others.

Paul told the Corinthians, "Be reconciled." This is also our message. We are called and empowered to invite others to be reconciled to God. We invite them to the deep truth of knowing God forgives us, accepts us, and cherishes us. New creation becomes a new outlook and a new way of life. It is a newness that embodies reconciliation "so that in him we might become the righteousness of God" (verse 21). As we are reconciled to God, we share in God's righteousness, which includes a constellation of divine attributes such as integrity, virtue, justice, purity of life, rightness, correctness of thinking feeling, and acting. Such righteousness is inherent in our new life. It is implanted in our hearts as we are reconciled to God through Jesus Christ.

How might that reconciliation change the way in which you approach your work and your relationships? Where do you think new creation through reconciliation needs to be experienced in our larger world?

NEW CHANCE
LUKE 15:1-3, 11b-32

The story in Luke 15:11-32 is traditionally called the story of the prodigal son. The parable epitomizes reconciliation and new beginnings. While the story is more correctly a story of a man and his two sons, we can use the word *prodigal* in its broader meaning to view the characters in the parable.

It is interesting that the word *prodigal* is not found in the Scripture verses themselves. The word means "excessively extravagant, lavish, and luxuriant." It is used to label the son who claimed his inheritance and wasted it by living as a spendthrift and reveler. It could also be used to describe the older brother, who, after discovering that his brother had come home, displayed excessive anger and jealousy because their father celebrated the younger son's return with a feast. However, the word may best describe the father.

The father divided his estate prior to his death to give to a son who wanted to leave. He waited for his younger son to come home from wandering. When he saw him, he ran and kissed his neck; clothed him with robes, a ring, and sandals; and threw a party to celebrate his homecoming. He received the anger of his older son and affirmed his action toward the younger son and his devotion to the older son as well. "Son, you are always with me, and all that is mine is yours. But we had to celebrate and rejoice, because this brother of yours was dead and has come to life; he was lost and has been found" (verses 31-32). The prodigal father's actions are excessively extravagant, lavish, and luxuriant in their expression of love.

What do we learn from the prodigal father in the story? Love is never divided up. Resurrection is a celebration. Reconciliation does not require terms, conditions, and treaties. From what we learn, we can imagine that the father waits for the older son to come home as well, to leave his anger behind, and to be reconciled.

Jesus told the story of the prodigals as a response to the grumbling of certain Pharisees and scribes who were offended because Jesus welcomed tax collectors and sinners. Granted, tax collectors were government thieves who charged individuals exorbitant amounts of money, gave a percentage to the government as that person's taxes, and kept the rest as a commission. Tax collectors were viewed as traitors and thieves. A prodigal Jesus taught about the good news of a prodigal God who would go to any length to bring the wandering son or daughter home.

Who, then, was the older son? Those who had appeared righteous all along, who had taken seriously their faith and their commitment to lead holy lives. The Pharisees and the scribes were respected and admired holy leaders of the faith community. To those among them who grumbled, Jesus offered a word of hope in the parable of a father who provided for both his sons.

Whenever we begin to think that God's love has limits, that God only will love those who fill a particular moral slot, or that God's grace is only open to those who act in a specifically holy or moral way, then the specter of the older son rises up and overshadows whatever good we might think we are doing. Imagine what would happen if we ran toward those who slowly make their way up the path to our church, embraced them, wrapped them in new robes, and celebrated their place in God's kingdom with a party. Imagine what would happen if we Christians gave away everything except the desire to invite others to begin again, without restrictions, without conditions, in order to find reconciliation in the arms of a loving God. Imagine what would happen in our families if we let go of jealousy and old grudges. Imagine what it would be like to find forgiveness and a new chance at reconciliation when we have been careless and thoughtless in our relationships. Jesus' parable comes alive because it invites all of us into reconciliation with God and neighbor. It invites us into the prodigal love of God.

Jesus leaves the story unfinished. We do not know how the older son will respond to the father. Like the older son, we can choose how we will make our lives the answer to the parable. When we see an opportunity for reconciliation to occur, we can respond with celebration or we can grumble. When we choose to keep others at arm's length or to punish them for how they have offended or hurt us, we place ourselves in a small, cold prison. We expend our energies trying to keep the walls of irreconcilable differences from crumbling.

Jesus' parable raises questions for all of us. How prodigal is our love for others? What conditions do we place on others in order to receive our love? Are we willing to learn how to live and love in the example of Christ? Our hearts may wander in a faraway country. Our hearts may stand with anger outside the doors of a homecoming celebration. In both cases, God's prodigal love offers us the opportunity for reconciliation and new life.

In what areas of your life do you need to experience the prodigal love of God? In what areas do you need to experience reconciliation and new life?

Transformation

Scriptures for Lent:
The Fifth Sunday
Isaiah 43:16-21
Philippians 3:4b-14
John 12:1-8

When our sons were little, I was secretly pleased about their lack of desire to try new or different foods. I know it is the responsibility of any good parent to expose the children to a wide range of nutritious foods. We did that; but the boys rejected Chinese food, seafood, steak, and a variety of other tasty menus. I wish I could say that it made me sad to think of them missing out on those delicious food types, but I knew that I could cook them up for me and there was no danger of what I would call "child-food tax," which is handing away a portion of my meal for the boys to taste. If they did not like it, they would not taste it.

Things changed as they grew up. They turned into human vacuum cleaners. They wanted some of all the delicious, pricey foods I dearly loved! As I blissfully steamed snow crab or grilled a t-bone, it often vanished before I had a chance to eat any of it. I demanded an explanation of how they could change the rules. Why were they now eating what they once absolutely refused to eat? My sons, at that point, would just smile and reach across the counter to snag the largest piece of whatever had been prepared and suck it down their esophagus like a Hoover with a new cleaner bag.

As I whined to my wife about this transformation, she responded, "They grew up, and everything has changed!" We had witnessed a sudden, clear, and irrevocable transformation of taste buds and stomach capacity.

While the transformation of our sons' eating habits is a light-hearted illustration, it is true that it had an effect on the entire family. Change is an everyday experience. Our Scriptures for this study connect us with three unique views of transformation that are brought about by our relationship with God. Take special note of the way in which a transformation not only changes the one transformed but also alters the world around the one who is transformed. Transformation always happens in relationships.

TRANSFORMING A PEOPLE
ISAIAH 43:16-21

When was the last time you did a truly new thing? Often, we do the same thing in a little different way or take on a hobby that is similar to what we have done before. When some of us succumb to midlife crises, instead of doing something completely new as a way of dealing with aging, we will take on variations of our former life. We buy a different car. We do a different job. We enter into a different relationship. Such changes are simply more of the same.

"I am about to do a new thing; / now it springs forth, do you not perceive it?" (verse 19), God's statement to the people of Israel was bold! Verses 16-21 delineate the act of salvation that God brought about by bringing the Israelites through the sea on dry land as they were being pursued by Pharaoh's chariots. God then destroyed Pharoah's army by bringing the floodwaters back upon then; and "chariot and horse, army and warrior" were extinguished (verse 17). It was the single most important event for the nation of Israel, for it proved to the world and to the Israelites that God was in charge. God's power was greater than Pharaoh's. God brought freedom and a new

life for the Israelites. Crossing the Red Sea was the first step of transformation into people of Israel. Their corporate memory continued from generation to generation as they told what God had done for them through the sacred meal of the Passover.

Imagine what a brash, prophetic statement it was to hear the prophet speak God's new word. "Do not remember the former things, or consider the things of old!" What? We should forget the Passover, the Red Sea, and the march to freedom from slavery? Nothing has ever been so important or will be so important for us again. We are known as the people who passed through the Flood. How could we ever forget that?"

"I will make a way in the wilderness, and rivers in the desert" (verse 19). Chapter 43 is addressed to the people who were in exile in Babylon. The time was drawing near for the return home after a captivity of nearly 70 years. God was not simply going to say they were free to return home. God was preparing a life-giving path and direction for them to follow. The new exodus would be safe. They would not suffer the hardships that they had suffered in the ancient exodus. Instead of complaining, thirst, hunger, and the death of a generation, God would lead the people through the wilderness with abundant water (verses 19-20). Instead of complaining, the people would praise God (verse 21). God's new thing would be a complete rescue of the people of God.

The other new thing, however, is more subtle and yet just as powerful when we identify it. The Jews believed that God had placed them in captivity as a consequence of forsaking God's covenant. The Jews left as a broken, distracted, disintegrated, saddened people. Their Temple was ruined, their worship fractured, and it seemed God had abandoned them. However, God was going to act to bring them home. God had no intention of bringing home the same distant and broken people who would not abide with a covenant. Isaiah says that God would "give drink to my chosen people, / the people whom I formed for myself, / so that they might declare my praise" (verses 20-21). The people would be re-integrated, reconnected with God, and transformed. They would be nothing like those who left. Yes, they were Jews whose ancestors walked through the Red Sea; but these would be transformed persons who understood that a relationship with God was to be cherished. A covenant with God was to be upheld by all means possible. A new, transformed people would be carried safely back to the land of Israel, to begin anew to know God in a focused and faithful way.

So what does this prophetic word mean for us who are living thousands of years later? Two important realizations are evident. First, we worship a God who reclaims, restores, and transforms us for new life and new paths of faithful journeying. God never lets us go. It is God's delight to see us transformed. Our own transformation may come after years of learning and waiting for God. We are transformed from brokenness to wholeness, from emptiness to purpose, from wandering to a new path, and from loneliness to community. God intends such things for you and me.

Second, God's "new thing," which made us a people, came in the person of Jesus Christ and continues to offer newness of life. We live in the possibility of what God may choose to accomplish for and with us as we live faithful and open lives, ready to serve and worship God. We live in God's living springs of hope.

How do you perceive and understand God's new thing in your life?

TRANSFORMING A HEART
PHILIPPIANS 3:4b-14

My father often used the phrase "wrongheaded." He used it with other words to create a significant word picture such as "wrongheaded numbskulls." He said things such as "Now, don't get so wrongheaded about what you are doing!" "That's just a plain wrongheaded way to look at things!" He used the word as a way to criticize; and if we think about the word (so long as we leave "numbskull" out of it), we can find value in what it teaches. It suggests to me that I am using the wrong, incorrect, or mistaken perspective as I look at an issue or a problem. Because I am starting out with the wrong tool—the wrong head—it is impossible for me to come a helpful conclusion. We can identify wrongheaded approaches in many areas: in politics, economics, cultural mores and practices, and personal relationships. We need to be careful in the use of the word, however, because an approach is not necessarily wrongheaded simply because it is different or does not agree with the approach of others. I would rather we use the word as a test for our own approach, our own perspective, or own heart's desire and focus. I can ask myself in honesty, discernment in a time of prayerful searching, "Am I being wrongheaded in this?" Such self-questioning can become a path to greater self-understanding.

Paul, in his letter to the Philippians, confessed his wrongheadedness. Before his conversion experience on the road to Damascus, his worth and status were carefully defined by what most of the Jewish world would have seen as a stellar pedigree. Paul described himself as "circumcised on the eighth day, a member of the people of Israel, of the tribe of Benjamin, a Hebrew born of Hebrews; as to the law, a Pharisee; as to zeal, a persecutor of the church; as to righteousness under the law, blameless" (verses 5-6). Paul said all of this gave him the right to be "confident in the flesh"(verse 4). That phrase reveals his understanding that he was wrongheaded. While it refers to circumcision in this letter, it also refers to perspectives based upon a vulnerable, human understanding.[1]

What is important in life and in the world of the Christian is not pedigree awards and status, and Paul confessed that. In verse 7, he was careful to lay all of that up against his new relationship with Christ: "Yet whatever gains I had, these I have come to regard as loss because of Christ" (verse 7). Now we begin to see a new approach of rightheadedness and Paul's understanding of a transformation in his heart from his previous views of what was important to his current understanding of Christ's presence and love. Paul said, "I regard everything as loss because of the surpassing value of knowing Christ Jesus my Lord" (verse 8).

I wonder how many of us would be rightheaded enough to make that kind of statement and mean it. Would we regard everything we have accomplished, all of our fine awards, our places in society, our wealth and possessions, our relationships, and more as loss? When we look carefully and consider what it means to know Jesus Christ as Lord, we place our accomplishments in perspective. We become rightheaded. We find a true transformation. We often try to fit Jesus into the rest of our life's stuff or to keep a balance between the lord-ship of Christ in our lives and the other things that we would like to accomplish. What would happen if we, like Paul, gave it all away and regarded everything else as "rubbish" (or "dung" in the King James Version) in order to gain a deeper and more abiding relationship with Christ?

Paul used the word *righteousness* in a transforming way as well. In the Jewish understanding, right-eousness came from obedience to the Law, in maintaining the sacrifices, the Levitical rules, to performing all that would be needed to seek forgiveness from sin. Paul said in verse 9 that he was no longer interested in being righteous "on my own" through the Law but wanted to rely solely on the new relationship with Jesus Christ that brought justification and forgiveness of sin—not because of what he had done but because of what God had done for him through Jesus Christ.

Paul continued communicating his understanding of the transformation in mind and heart into a rightheadedness, although it is a way that the rest of the world may see as nonsensical. "I want to know Christ and the power of his resurrection and the sharing of his sufferings by becoming like him in his death" (verse 10). Paul was willing to suffer like Christ, for the sake of Christ, so as to know the hope of resurrection that came from him.

Paul issued to the Philippians, and offers to us, a bold and challenging way of looking at our own lives and our own understanding of salvation. It is not what we do but rather what Christ has already done. Our work is to come to know Christ and the gift of salvation more and more clearly. Such knowledge and the way of life it inspires is the goal of the transforming life in Christ. I say *transforming* and not *transformed* because it is an ongoing process of growing in our awareness and understanding of the gift Christ brings. Paul compared the process to an athletic event: "I press on toward the goal for the prize of the heavenly call of God in Christ Jesus" (verse 14). Growing in Christ was a goal worthy of giving away everything and anything that might hold him back from fully knowing Christ.

How shall we live? Who shall we be? What shall we hold as most valuable and precious in life? What would we even give our lives for? To be able to respond to all of these challenging questions understanding the grace of Christ, the gift of salvation, and the call to live a holy and loving life as a response to the grace of Christ is our "high calling," too.

How do you understand a transformed, rightheaded approach to life? What, if anything, stands in the way of your ability to "press on toward the goal for the prize of the heavenly call of God in Christ Jesus"?

TRANSFORMING A PURPOSE
JOHN 12:1-8

Jesus knew he was going to be killed. He knew that the plot against him was growing. Passover would soon arrive, and the city of Jerusalem was beginning to fill with pilgrims. There was no better place to be in the entire world than in Jerusalem for Passover. The last thing the religious authorities wanted was a giant scene that might draw Rome's attention and create chaos and unrest. Little did the priests know that the next morning Jesus would ride into Jerusalem on a young donkey with shouts of "Hosanna! / Blessed is the one who comes in the name of the Lord— / the King of Israel!" (verse 13). But that was tomorrow's work. The best thing Jesus could do at present was to find a place where he would be among friends. He traveled to Bethany.

Bethany is about two miles from Jerusalem, on the other side of the Mount of Olives. Jesus went to the home of his dear friends Martha, Mary, and Lazarus. He had raised Lazarus from the dead, so there was already a sense of awe and holiness surrounding the home. He was welcomed warmly, and his friends prepared a supper for Jesus and the other disciples.

John was specific about details of the meal. Martha served, and Lazarus was at the table with Jesus. At the meal, Mary offered a strange gesture. Instead of a simple, routine footwashing to take the dust and dirt off Jesus' feet after a day's walk, she anointed Jesus' feet with expensive perfume. She took a container of incredibly expensive perfume, the cost of which was the equal of a year's pay for a laborer at that time, poured the perfume on Jesus' feet, and wiped it with her own hair.

Scripture says that Judas was furious at the apparent waste of such resources. It further condemns Judas by saying that he was the treasurer and would often steal from the common purse (verses 5-6). Judas roundly criticized Mary for the extravagance. What a waste of a valuable piece of property, an asset that could be used for the poor or the needy! It is easy to take Judas's side. Wasn't it the ministry of Jesus to care for the poor, to see to those who had not enough? Isn't that the work of the church today, and don't we try to use our funds and resources so that the most good can come from our gifts? Honestly, why would Mary do such a wasteful thing?

However, Jesus stopped Judas's criticism cold and, in doing so, transformed Mary's simple act into something of much greater meaning and value. The true purpose in her act is revealed in Jesus' words to his complaining disciples. Jesus knew he was going to die. The traditional work of the women in a family at the time of death was to prepare the body for burial. They applied spices, scents, and balms. Jesus used the occasion to announce his pending death and burial. She had applied the nard as a gift of love, adoration, and tender honor and did so prior to his death to come. Instead of wasting it by pouring it on Jesus' feet, she prepared Jesus for his own death and burial in a loving and open manner. The incident prefigures Jesus' burial and Jesus' washing the feet of the disciples at the last supper.[2]

Imagine yourself as Mary for a moment. Do you expect she was concerned that the value and purpose of her action would be misconstrued? Or can we imagine that, for Mary, it really did not matter what others thought, that the anointing was an act of devotion and preparation for what was to come? By her actions, she transformed the purpose of the burial preparation to an act of love. In contrast to Judas's ultimate betrayal, Mary's actions demonstrate faithful discipleship.[3]

The story in John in this study is less a story of how we should take care of the poor as much as it is a story of how our actions make a difference in life in a wide variety of ways. For what seemed to be waste became an offering; and what seemed to be thoughtlessness became a deep, treasured gift. How do we approach the gifts and actions of others who come into our lives? Are we willing to accept and try to understand the gifts that they bring even if sometimes their gifts are hard to understand or may be what we think are inappropriate?

In a church I served, there was a young fellow in his twenties who was born with Down's syndrome. He lived and worked in a special residential center. He always came to worship and sat at the back of the church. Whenever he saw me, he spoke nearly at the top of his lungs. When I started to walk toward the pulpit at the beginning of the service, Robert would yell, "Hi, Pastor Randy! How are you today?" It became a regular call to worship for those who sat around him. It also was an embarrassing remark, because my name seemed to sound at the top of his greeting: RANDY! And it was also true that the meaning and purpose of that greeting was felt so deep in his heart that it could have as well been couched in the words, "Peace be with you. The Lord is with you, and also with me."

When we are able to respond thoughtfully to the actions of others, when we seek the meaning instead of quickly discounting the value and worth of an act because it does not quite fit, we open our heart and minds to the transforming power of Christ.

How might Mary's actions guide you in your life of faith and discipleship? How might she inspire your actions toward those who need love and care?

---

[1] From the note for Philippians 3:3 in *The New Interpreter's Study Bible*, page 2104.
[2] From *The New Interpreter's Bible*, Vol. IX; pages 702-03.
[3] From the note for John 12:4-6 in *The New Interpreter's Study Bible*, pages 1932-33.

Servanthood

Scriptures for Lent:
The Sixth Sunday
Isaiah 50:4-9a
Philippians 2:5-11
Luke 22:14–23:56

I have never pursued a career in food service. The closest I came to it was working as a donut fryer in Dallas during my last semester of seminary. I was in the back room making the donuts and rarely saw the customers. I am not sure I would have been able to listen to a table full of orders and make sure everyone had the right meal before them! I respect and feel a bit sorry for food service workers. They often suffer abuse from the customer if an order is not quite right or the food comes out too rare or too well done or there is mustard on the hamburger. They are often ignored as though they are merely part of the scenery. I have been to dinner with people who normally are caring and courteous persons; but when they have a waiter or a waitress in front of them, they begin to act like the king or queen of the realm. They bark out commands rather than courteous requests. Often the customer offers no eye contact, no gentleness in the voice, and a real sense that they are more important than the one serving. I feel sad when acquaintances treat servers with disdain.

In our Scriptures for this session, we come face to face with servants who are placed in difficult and dangerous situations. We will see servanthood in the themes of trust, humility, and redemption as we live out this week of palms and passion in preparation for the Easter celebration.

TRUST
ISAIAH 50:4-9a

Trust is a powerful word. Imagine all the things you trust in your life. Think of what you take for granted that will always be there, that will be consistent, steady, and normal. Trust nurtures relationships of all kinds. We trust doctors to treat our illnesses. We trust pilots to carry us safely to our destinations. Children trust parents to provide for them. Spouses in a healthy marriage trust one another's loyalty and support. We trust driving rules, water from the faucet, electricity. We trust that the systems we need for our work will function properly. Sometimes, intentionally or unintentionally, our trust is betrayed; yet we know that without such trust, we will not be able to function in everyday life. Persons with deep psychological struggles are often those with a deep-seated mistrust of daily life.

Trust means to accept the promise of another. We give away control over at least a piece of our lives with the faith that what will happen by another's hand will benefit and not harm. When trust functions well, health and strength abound. When trust is betrayed, we suffer. We are wounded by suspicion and uncertainty.

Isaiah 50:4-9 is often referred to as the third Servant Song of Isaiah. The servant songs are particular writings that talk about an individual or the nation of Israel as one who carries either the good news or the pain of the salvation for Israel. In Chapter 42, the first verses present "my servant" who will bring justice to the nations. In Chapter 50, we have a picture of one like a prophet who suffers in the process of listening to and trusting God.

Many students of the Bible read the servant songs in light of the life, ministry, and suffering of Jesus. Christians look to Isaiah and understand Jesus the Messiah as God's suffering servant. I think it is helpful to look at Isaiah's writings and realize that Jesus indeed did go through things similar to what the servant is described as enduring. It helps me to see that Jesus' life and suffering were like that described in the servant songs. Jesus himself quoted Isaiah to help describe his own mission and ministry (Luke 4:18-19).

However, the material in Isaiah was written centuries before Jesus, and I think it is also important to imagine these words apart from the New Testament and Jesus' life and to consider what they meant for the people of Israel in captivity in Babylon who would soon return home to Israel. How is God present with Israel? What can we learn about suffering? Such reflection can deeply enrich our understanding of God's presence in the lives of God's people and in Jesus.

The servant in Chapter 50 has been taught by God and is a teacher who has the mission of sustaining the weary. The servant is also a student who continues to listen to God's voice and instruction in order to share it with others. Wouldn't we all hope to have the same role? Don't we hope to continue to grow in our faith that we might bring faith and strength to others? It is exciting to experience new insights during Bible study and personal devotion and to talk about them with others.

However, the work of the servant goes beyond teaching and

learning. Something appears to be wrong. The servant was living in the midst of a painful situation. Even as the servant brought comfort to Israel, they treated him horribly. The treatment may have come because of the servant's words. Perhaps they were too hard to hear. You know how it is sometimes when someone speaks the truth in love but the truth is almost too much to bear. We become angry with the one who would speak those words to us. The treatment given to the servant probably says more about Israel's fear and struggle to make sense of its own suffering in Babylon than the anger at the words of the servant.

Whatever the case, the physical abuse and harm was horrendous. The servant was beaten on his back. His beard was torn out by the roots. He was spit on and insulted. Anyone who would see him would infer that he had done a terrible wrong to be treated this way and that justice was being served by this punishment being poured out on him! He stood in total disgrace to the outside world. What was his crime? Teaching and sustaining the weary with a word.

Can you remember times in your life, when your good was treated poorly? Have you tried to do what was right and honorable and people reacted in a way that was the complete opposite of what you expected? Have people criticized you when all you did was try to care by bringing truth to the struggle? It happens more often than we would think. We shoot the messenger who brings the truth we cannot bear. If I were the servant, honestly, I would find a new line of work. I would leave for a foreign land and probably shake the dust off my shoes. If those people cannot hear the truth of God, then best of wishes; and have a nice life!

The servant was much more faithful to God than I am, for he knew his work and ministry was focused on what God wanted and not simply on the reaction of the people. When we speak the truth, even in love, we often can expect a reaction that is sometimes as painful as our words. The servant received that and more. Notice, however, the servant's faith. "The Lord GOD helps me; / therefore I have not been disgraced; / therefore I have set my face like flint, / and I know that I shall not be put to shame; / he who vindicates me is near" (verses 7-8). These words point to trust in the midst of affliction. Beaten, torn, abused, and degraded, yet his spirit stood strong and faithful. His trust in God did not waver.

We are rarely confronted with such a challenge to our faith. Unfortunately, we sometimes crumble instead of finding faith in the God who never abandons us. It makes a huge difference in our ability to be faithful when we prepare ourselves daily in prayer and in discernment of God's will and call. It is good to ask ourselves about the depth of our well of trust in God. How strong can we stand when faced with the abuse of the world as we try to act in love, justice, and honesty? Do we truly know that God helps us as we listen carefully to God's teachings and guidance? How different would our world, our church, our families, and our lives be if we, like the suffering servant in Isaiah 50, would trust in God at all times, even during times of affliction?

What are some of the difficult times in your life? How was God present for you during those times?

HUMILITY
PHILIPPIANS 2:5-11

Humble. Humility. Humiliation. All three words come from an interesting Latin root: *humus.* Of course, those of you who are gardeners or farmers know that word well. It means "dirt." *Humus* is the soil, the rich earth out of which things grow. We can think of it as the mud out of which God formed the first human being and blew into him the breath of life (Genesis 2:7). The word *humiliation* is related to *humus.* To be humiliated is to be brought back down to the earth. A Catholic priest or nun, in taking their vows of obedience, will lie prostrate on the floor—in a sense, in the *humus*—in order to take on a new life of openness to God's leading. The meaning is also

in the word *humble.* Humble people may take their life's work seriously, but they take themselves lightly. They see that the most important thing is not to make sure the camera and spotlights are shining on their faces but on the good thing that is being produced.

I think Philippians may be Paul's best letter. No, it is not as theologically intricate at Romans nor as contentious as Corinthians; but in terms of its ability to paint a picture for our faith in a wide range of experiences, I believe it wins. "Let the same mind be in you that was in Christ Jesus" (4:5). Think for a moment if that were the only verse of Scripture you had to meditate on. It contains a lifetime of discernment and thought. Take everything you think, believe, and understand about yourself, about the world, and even the way in which you think and form opinions and decisions and set them aside. Now "take up the mind of Christ Jesus." Conform and mold all that you are after Christ's way of thought. In the next three verses, Paul described the mind of Christ Jesus as he took human form. Paul said he "emptied himself" (2:7). Christ "did not regard equality with God as something to be exploited" (verse 6). He took on "the form of a slave, being born in human likeness" (verse 7). What a change Christ made for our sake. Paul said that Christ "humbled himself" (verse 8). The Greek word that is translated "humbled" means "to make low or to bring low." He was obedient to the point of death—"even death on a cross" (verse 8). In terms of salvation experience, Paul minced no words. He did not talk about what a good teacher Jesus was or about the miracles he performed or anything that might distract from the essential message of salvation: Christ was God. He humbled himself to humanity and then to death as an ultimate gift of self-denial for our sake.

Verses 9-11 are a glimpse of Easter. "Therefore," Paul said, because of all that had happened, hear the good news. Because of Christ's willingness to empty himself, to humble himself, to be obedient to death, God brought him to the highest exaltation. We find a doxology in Paul's writing: that Jesus' name would be above all names, that all would humble themselves on their knees before this one who gave himself for all, that all would address and acknowledge the lordship of Jesus Christ to God's glory. Christ's humility is more than simply an example for us to follow. It became the route to salvation, the route that led to the reconciliation of the world to God and the recovery of holy and hopeful life for all humanity.

How do you understand humility? How might the practice of humility enrich your life of faith? What role might it play in your speech, your actions, your decisions, your lifestyle, and your interaction with the world?

REDEMPTION
LUKE 22:14–23:56

This session's Scripture from Luke is huge. This passage contains 114 verses to study! Yet it is a portion of Scripture that invites us to enter the story of Christ's last hours on earth. I think one of the more powerful aspects of this story from Luke is the fact that it simply tells the story. Luke does not "theologize" or talk about the meaning of Jesus' death. Instead, the story is simply shared with us; and we are left to reflect upon the power and depth of the Crucifixion. Of course, that is true for our entire faith. We hear the story; and we are invited to think, to meditate, and to come to a faithful conclusion: "Here is the life of Jesus Christ. We believe he lived and died for our redemption."

Luke 22:14–23:56 offers vivid details about the Last Supper; the dispute about greatness; the prediction of Peter's denial; instructions about purse, bag and sword; the prayer on the Mount of Olives; betrayal and arrest; Peter's denial; mocking and beating; Jesus before the council, Pilate, and Herod; the death sentence; the Crucifixion; the death; and the burial. It is critical that we prayerfully read these Scriptures that form the basis for worship during the season of Lent. As we re-enter the events in Luke's story, we begin to grasp a fuller sense of Jesus' servanthood and the redemptive power of God.

The details of Jesus' death in Luke 23:44-49 offer rich images that can help us understand God's redemption. First, the world became dark. We cannot be sure if it simply became so darkly clouded that it appeared night or whether there was an eclipse; but for three hours, the world took on the aspect of a tomb. Darkness certainly reminds us of what it was like before God spoke the first word at Creation. All was a swirling void before God said, "Let there be light." At Jesus' death, the world plunged again into darkness.

Second, "the curtain of the temple was torn in two." Exodus 26:31-35 describes a curtain that was prepared for the Tabernacle in the wilderness. The ark of the covenant, which signified the presence of God, was placed behind the curtain. It was believed that God resided permanently in the darkness of the Holy of Holies.[1] Tearing the curtain opened the holiest place on the earth for the Jews to the outside world. The imagery is powerful as Christ was torn on the cross so holiness could spread to the world.

Finally, Christ spoke his last words. "Father, into your hands I commend my spirit" (23:46). These words quote Psalm 31:5, which says, "Into your hand I commit my spirit you have redeemed me, O LORD, faithful God." These details—darkness, the torn curtain in the Temple, and the last words of Jesus—underscore the redemptive power of God at work in the death of Jesus.

As we consider all three of our Scripture selections for this session, we recognize again the theme of servanthood found in all of them. Isaiah gives us the image of one who remained a faithful servant of God even in the face of brutality and pain. Paul tells us the story of the Christ, who, although the same as God, humbled himself as a servant and became obedient to the work of salvation on the cross. Finally, in Luke we find the narratives of Jesus' death, all of which demonstrate his willingness to serve God and humanity.

Some persons like to ask the question, "What would Jesus do?" as a way of making decisions in life. Many of the answers come out of Scripture quotations such as "Do to others as you would have them do to you" (Luke 6:31) or "Love one another" (John 13:34). Those are fine answers and a good way to live an ethical and caring life. However, I believe the best answer is that Jesus would have us act as servants for the sake of others and, thus, participate in and share God's love and redemption.

How can your life reflect focused, intentional servanthood? Who in your life would benefit from your gift of servanthood in the name of Christ?

---

[1] From *Harper's Bible Dictionary* (Harper-Collins, 1985); page 64.

Resurrection: New Beginnings

Scriptures for Easter:
Acts 10:34-43
1 Corinthians 15:19-26
John 20:1-18

Easter is all about new beginnings. In this sense, it reminds me of our family celebration of New Year's Eve. In the last 15 seconds of the year, I herd the family to the front door. As we count down the passing of the old year, we stand in the door with pots, spoons, and noisemakers in hand, ready for action. We greet the new year with honks, rattles, and bangs, with as much noise as we can make. Our noise celebrates the opportunity to begin something new. Certainly, much of who we are and what we do does not change; but at least a little something is different even if it is only the date on the calendar. I love a new start.

Easter morning, like New Year's morning, is always fresh with life. Perhaps we should greet it with noisemaking in the way we greet the new year because Easter offers us a chance to say, "Now we begin." That is why Scripture selections for this session of Easter Sunday captivate me. Each one of them opens doors to a new beginning!

A NEW WITNESS
ACTS 10:34-43

One of my jobs in The United Methodist Church is to serve as superintendent of a district in the Dakotas Conference. We share the Dakotas with a large number of Native Americans, and our lives and traditions have a profound impact on each other's cultures. We also have a growing number of immigrants who are settling in our larger communities. The people in the rural Dakotas, however, have traditionally understood themselves by their northern European ancestry.

We have been blessed with a growing number of Korean United Methodist clergy in our area. They bring devotion, competency, and enthusiasm. I enjoy the reactions and responses of predominantly Caucasian rural churches to the prospect of having a Korean person as their pastor. In almost every circumstance, the response of people has been, "Well, they seem nice enough; and it might be good for us to stretch ourselves a little! We will work on understanding their English better and follow where they lead us." Some of these statements were coming from churches that just over 50 years ago had worship services that were not in English. Most of their services were in German or another European language. The openness of the people reflects their desire to have a good solid pastor leading them no matter who they are or what they look like. It is a testament to their willingness to look at the spirit of Christ within one another.

Each time we recognize the inherent worth and value of another culture, we open new doors. We enter new places where the witness to the resurrection of Christ may occur. It is a beautiful moment in church history when that happens, for the true understanding of the universal offer of salvation becomes evident as we reach out to another culture and as another culture reaches out to us.

The Christian faith emerged from the Jewish faith. Acts 10 describes events that opened Peter's eyes and heart to a broader understanding of who might be included among those who follow Jesus Christ. Peter was a faithful Jew. Born in Galilee, he attended to the law of Moses even as he fol-

lowed the One he believed to be the Messiah. The Law was fulfilled in this Messiah, and they continued to worship at the Temple even while they worshiped and celebrated the resurrection of Jesus. Had the faith remained within the Jewish faith, however, and had it not opened its arms to Gentiles or non-Jews, the world would be quite different today.

The Spirit of God could not be contained in one religion. Acts 10 begins with the story of Peter and Cornelius, who was a Roman centurion. Cornelius was a "God-fearer," one who worshiped God and was friendly to the Jewish faith. Scripture tells us that he prayed and gave alms (verses 1-2).

Cornelius was praying, as was his custom, and received a vision from God in the form of an angel who told him to contact Peter in Joppa. The next day, Peter had a vision in which he heard the voice of God three times telling him to eat food that was considered unclean in Jewish dietary laws. God said, "What God has made clean, you must not call profane" (verse 15). As Peter puzzled over the meaning of the vision, Cornelius's messengers appeared and invited Peter to visit Cornelius's home and speak to him. Peter went with them. During the initial encounter, Peter discovered for himself and articulated the meaning of his vision: "God has shown me that I should not call anyone profane or unclean" (verse 28). This was a stretch for Peter. He who was faithful within one framework of faith had to take the power of the Resurrection and look beyond the traditional laws regarding non-Jews in order to see and meet a new audience. Cornelius shared the miraculous story of his own vision from God and said, "All of us are here in the presence of God to listen to all that the Lord has commanded you to say" (verse 33).

Peter shared his expanded understanding of the Christian faith. He began with a bold new statement: "I truly understand that God shows no partiality, but in every nation anyone who fears him and does what is right is acceptable to him" (verses 34-35). He retold God's activity in Jesus in the ministry, death, and resurrection of Jesus. He shared a promise offered by God to all people—Jew and non-Jew. "Everyone who believes in him receives forgiveness of sins through his name" (verse 43).

Can you understand Easter and resurrection in this Scripture? The truth of Jesus Christ's resurrection opened doors that had been culturally closed. Peter tried to be as faithful as possible. (He was called "the rock" on which Christ would build the church.) As the experience with Cornelius demonstrated, Peter came to realize that the most faithful thing he could do was to preach to whomever had ears to hear the good news.

Our world is torn by conflict, much of which originates because of cultural and religious differences. The Easter message in Acts 10:34-43 calls all of us to a renewed way of thinking about the meaning of Christ. It calls us to become like Peter in our willingness to cross cultural boundaries and like Cornelius in our willingness to listen to one another.

What cultural or religious barriers exist in your life? How might Peter's words break down such barriers? What new life might happen?

A NEW HOPE
1 CORINTHIANS 15:19-26

My father died in 1993 when I was 36 years old. He died of cancer, like so many; but his diagnosis was mysterious for most of his illness. In fact, it was only in the last two days of his life that the doctors became convinced that they could say that cancer was the cause; but by then, it did not matter. My tall, towering, always in charge, retired Air Force lieutenant colonel, wise father died. Did he live a good life? For the most part, yes, although perhaps haunted by the images of two different wars that he fought in and many other things in his life that he perhaps did not accomplish the way he wanted. I would say he had a pretty good life and that it was better than most lives in the world. He was married to the same woman for 44 years and had seven children and many grandchildren. He was healthy for most of his life until the end. He had freedom to travel in his work and, thus, had seen most of the world. In many ways it was a good life.

However, even when I consider all that he did, it seems to me that he died too young. I think of what might have happened for him had he lived longer than 65 years. The memory of Roger Cross, while vital in the minds and hearts of those who loved him, is a tiny footnote in the history of humankind. When I think of my ancestors further back in time, if I even know a name and when they lived and died, I know little about their life goals and passions. The overwhelming majority of the people of this world are gently forgotten through the ages. We are, and then we were, and then the world travels on and leaves us there.

What a bleak and empty view of life on this celebration of Easter! That is exactly the point Paul stated in First Corinthians, "If for this life only we have hoped in Christ, we are of all people most to be pitied" (15:19). We may not believe in the Resurrection; but, instead, we see our faith as something to help us get by during our time on earth. We may believe that Jesus saved us from our sin but that when we die all is done. We live for 65 years and try to be good people; but we may believe that when we are dead, all is over. We may live our lives selfishly and then die; and in a few generations, no one remembers us.

If death is the final answer, why live a faithful life? What is the point? If death separates us from the love of God in Christ Jesus our Lord, then death appears to have more power than our faith could ever muster. If this were the case, Paul was right. We who try to be faithful, who place our trust in Christ ought to be most pitied. If this life is all there is, then like the Epicureans of the Roman times we should live only for the total pleasure of life, for at the end of it, at least we have had fun.

The good news of Easter is that there is more to life. With the resurrection of Christ from the dead comes new hope for each of us, hope for our life from day to day and hope beyond death. Paul said, "Christ has been raised from the dead, the first fruits of those who have died" (verse 20). In Jesus Christ, God's Son, a new chapter in the history of God's relationship with the world opens. It is a chapter of victory through life in Jesus Christ.

We have been ruled by disease, famine, poverty, war, conflict and strife, the power of living a hard life, and not seeing anything beyond hardship. Many of us fear death. It lords over us like a pervasive, all-knowing force. It drives us to anxiety and fear. It changes the way in which we can trust. It limits our capacity to risk standing up for others. We could die, and it scares us to death.

In spite of the power of such rulers in our lives, we have hope. Christians look death in the eye and believe that Christ is more powerful than death. Our life is held in the hands of the One who has brought new hope to us in Christ. Christ is risen from the dead. Death has no power over Christ or over God's will and love for us. Christ's resurrection places him in power; and the time will come when all those other powers that we fear will be destroyed, and Christ will hand the kingdom to God (verse 24).

Paul's good news about the Resurrection is the good news of Easter. We are more than death by the gift of Jesus Christ, and what we do today does make an eternal difference. We are called and invited to live in the power of resurrection in all that we say, do, and think as we follow the One who has brought hope and eternal life.

What thoughts or feelings do you have about death? about resurrection? How does the resurrection of Christ offer hope in your life?

NEW LIFE
JOHN 20:1-18

Preparing youth to do a sunrise service is a terrible joy. I use the oxymoron "terrible joy" because the work is so hard and the event so important. The task of helping youth understand the seriousness and the joy of receiving the news of resurrection on Easter often drives pastors and youth leaders to distraction on the days before Easter. I remember one year when I had a group of funny, entertaining youth. Throughout the rehearsal for the service, the more I tried to get them to focus, the more they flew off in their imagination to the four corners of the earth. In frustration and exhaustion, I finally ended the rehearsal early and wished them all good luck on Easter. I hoped they would not embarrass themselves and their families by not being prepared. Like Pontius Pilate, I washed my hands of them. It was not the way I had hoped to prepare for Easter Day

When Easter morning, came I dreaded the first event. I hoped no one would show up and that the ill-prepared service would fade into oblivion. It was a particularly nice morning, and the sunrise service had twice as many people as usual in it. All I could see was a gathering darkness. I tried to look into the eyes of the youth before the service, but I saw no hint of fear or concern. I resigned myself to a bad experience. Everyone appeared to be in place for their various leadership roles.

I looked up front and saw our "lead off" youth at the pulpit. He was one of the youngest members of the group and was in charge of the Easter greeting. As the lights came up, he yelled at the top of his squeaky, high boy-soprano voice, "Christ is risen!" Laughter bellowed from the members of the congregation because they did not expect that first sound. Quiet again, he continued, "Christ is risen!" Finally people began to hear the muffled sounds of the youth up front who were responding to the ancient Easter greeting with "He is risen indeed." It was a quiet, sleepy rising; but the words were exchanged. However, the youth leader was not satisfied. He yelled again, "Christ is Risen!" The congregation responded, "He is risen indeed." Over and over again came the yell from the pulpit as the congregation's voice grew louder and more enthusiastic. Finally, at the last, the sound was so thundering between the speaker and the smiling faces of the worshipers that you could have almost rolled a stone away. Easter had come, and the announcement of new life had been shared with a squeaky voice that would not be silent until the world had responded.

John 20:1-18 is my favorite version of the events of the first Easter. The narrative is full of vivid details. Mary came to the tomb early Sunday morning, the first day of the week, and found the stone rolled away. Without even looking, she ran to Simon Peter and the other disciple, perhaps waking them up to tell them her fear: "They have taken the Lord." That is the context in which Peter ran to the tomb to see for sure if what Mary had said was true. The two disciples went inside the place of death and saw only rags. "Then the other disciple, who reached the tomb first, also went in, and he saw and believed; for as yet they did not understand the scripture, that he must rise from the dead" (verses 8-9).

The truth emerges in the next part of the narrative. Mary wept and bent over to look again into the tomb. She saw two angels who questioned her tears and her sadness: "Woman, why are you weeping?" (verse 13). The angels understood what Mary did not, that Jesus had risen from the dead. She turned around and came face to face with Jesus, yet she was so filled with death and hopelessness that she could not truly see him. She thought he was the gardener. She asked him about Jesus' body. As we look in this story, we see the truth; but only at this point does new life emerge for Mary and for the world.

Jesus spoke her name: "Mary." The first word of the resurrected Christ was to call the first disciple of the new chapter in human history by her name. She recognized his voice, and her life was surely raised from the dead. She was renewed, resurrected from hopelessness, and offered a new role: "Go to my brothers and say to them, 'I am ascending to my Father and your Father, to my God and your God'" (verse 17). Mary became the first evangelist of the Christian faith on Easter morning; and you know she ran and told them all, "I have seen the Lord."

The story invites us to consider important questions. Are we walking in death or in life today? Do we believe we have a new life in Christ? Do we honestly believe that resurrection life, begun in Christ, is part of our lives now? Or do we stand outside the tomb of past failures and lost dreams and wait for Someone to speak our names? Mary and the disciples had nothing left except to prepare a dead body with burial spices or to huddle in a room with the doors locked for fear of the authorities who would rout out the rest of the rebels to Rome and the Jewish Temple. Mary heard Jesus speak her name, and then nothing else mattered. She proclaimed, "I have seen the Lord" (verse 18).

"Christ is risen!" The proclamation resonates on Easter. "He is risen indeed!" Our response heralds new life and hope for all people.

What would it mean to you to hear the risen Christ speak your name? What does it mean to you to proclaim "Christ is risen!"?